Simple Family Worship

**A Christian Commonplace Book**

*Simple Family Worship*

Simple Family Worship

Zack Fink

# ORDINARY PUBLISHING

Ordinary Publishing House
Phoenix, Arizona

Simple Family Worship

Ordinary Publishing House
1706 E Harwell Road, Phoenix AZ 85042

www.ordinarypublilshing.com

© 2021 Zack Fink

All rights reserved, including the right to reproduce this book or portions thereof in any form whatsoever, except in the case of brief quotations embodied in articles or reviews. Guidelines provided by the United States of America copyright law. For permissions contact:

ordinarypublishing@gmail.com


For other information, corrections, feedback, questions or concerns, please contact the author at zackfink.com.


First Edition
Soft copy ISBN: 978-1-956743-00-5

Scripture quotations are from;
The Holy Bible, English Standard Version® (ESV®)
Copyright © 2001 by Crossway, a publishing ministry of Good News Publishers. All rights reserved. ESV Text Edition: 2016.

Creed quotations from;
Creeds. (2018, October 03). Retrieved September 19, 2020, from https://www.crcna.org/welcome/beliefs/creeds. Used by permission of Faith Alive Christian Resources.

The Children's Catechism quotations from
Historic Church Documents. (n.d.).
Retrieved September 19, 2020, from
https://reformed.org/historic-confessions/the-childrens-catechism

For my Family

## TABLE OF CONTENTS

| | |
|---|---|
| Forward | 11 |
| Family Worship: A Primer | 14 |
| Bible Reading | 25 |
| Prayer | 27 |
| Creeds | 33 |
| The Children's Catechism | 41 |
| Scripture | 59 |
| Singing | 81 |
| Appendix | 85 |

Forward

Isaac Ambrose was a Puritan of special gifting.  His writing, especially his book "Looking to Jesus," has long held its own in popular appreciation with the writings of John Bunyan."[1]   His book, "MEDIA: The Middle Things," had a tremendous influence on me.  Actually, to appreciate the book, you should also know its lengthy sub-title: "MEDIA: The Middle Things or The Means, Duties, Ordinances, Secret, Private and Public, for continuance and increase of a Godly Life, (once begun) until we come to heaven."[2]

The "Middle Things" dealt with everything that occurs in our lives between our salvation and our inevitable earthly deaths.  Ambrose spends 150 or so pages outlining the nature of our experiences, evidences, and particularly, our family duties.  And as a good Puritan, he spends a considerable amount of effort promoting spiritual disciplines such as teaching us how to prepare to hear the Word of God, how we should prepare to receive the sacraments, how we should approach the reading of the Scriptures, and preparation for fasting and prayer.

No serious Christian argues against developing such discipline in both our lives and the lives of our children, yet we often fall short.  Those two all-to-familiar foes, Disorder and Time, strive together to undermine our best efforts.  Thankfully, we have a guide like "Simple Family Worship" to provide for us a streamlined, yet well-structured devotion time.  Modelled carefully after the elements of worship, this "How-To" guide provides easy to follow instructions to make instituting and, moreover, sustaining family devotions a snap.  This book give us a choice.  Day after day, we can repeatedly gather together a fair and diverse collection of resources we need or we can pick-up "Simple Family Worship" as our one-stop solution.  For me, easier is always better and I wish that I would have had a tool like this one back when my children were young.

Ease of use aside, my favorite aspect of "Simple Family Worship" is the upbeat tone. 1 Peter 2:9 says: "But you are a chosen people, a royal priesthood, a holy nation, a people belonging to God, that you may declare the praises of him who called you out of darkness into his wonderful light. Once you were not a people, but now you are the people of God; once you had not received mercy, but now you have received mercy." This verse reinforces to us our new status within the Kingdom; we are a royal priesthood. Thus, conforming to the image of Christ for us is not drudgery or a chore, but a privilege of position. Instead of viewing our discipleship, including our family worship, as a chore or a duty, "Simple Family Worship" embraces the spirit and tone of 1 John 5:3. Because we love Christ, we choose to keep His commandments not out of burden or chore, but out of sheer devotion. "Simple Family Worship" captures the understanding that parents exercises the discipleship of their children out of gratitude and faithfulness - rather than duty. I hope it blesses you as it has our family.

Vic Fink
2020

Family Worship: A Primer

"And if it is evil in your eyes to serve the Lord, choose this day whom you will serve, whether the gods your fathers served in the region beyond the River, or the gods of the Amorites in whose land you dwell. But as for me and my house, we will serve the Lord."

Joshua 24:15

## Start Today

Any family wanting to worship God daily can and should. This is a practical, hands-on guide and resource, for the head of the family. In many cases, this is the husband or father. In some cases this is the mom or someone else. That is not to say the head of the family is the only person responsible for keeping the family accountable to worship. All members of the family should keep each other accountable. But, there are some solid Biblical arguments for the Father, if present, leading family worship. (Gen 12:3, Zech 12:10-14)

There are no special dispensations, tips, or tricks. To hold family worship in your home, you simply need to practice what you already know from your Church.

This primer will discuss what, why, how, when, and where to do family worship. More than that, it is the book you can use to lead your family. There are scriptures, creeds, prayers, and signing guidance to have a productive and effective way to worship God.

If you take one message away, it would be, "start today, right now, as soon as you are able." If you read and agree to just that statement and you are comfortable leading without the guidance of this book, I have achieved my goal.

Start today, add it to your daily family routines. Pick up the habit, no matter how challenging, awkward, strange, or unwieldy it might feel.

Giving God our attention, praise, focus, and offerings are how the Holy Spirit breathes grace into our lives. Family worship is one of the many ways Christians can walk the talk and live faithfully.

We are not christians just on Sunday. Embracing family worship honors God, his church, and our family's journey in Gospel truth and understanding.

Regular reading of God's word, real time discussions of what was read in the Bible, and prayer about how the Bible applies to our lives, all work in "step with the Holy Spirit." (Gal 5:25)

Enjoy the time set aside for regular worship. It's God honoring and precious family time. ( 1 Sam 2:30)

What is family worship?

Family worship is simply giving our time and attention to the work of Christ. It reminds us that worship does not start or end when we leave our church building.

We are simply mirroring what we do on Sunday in our church, just in a microcosm within our family. In family worship:

- We read the Bible and discuss the truths and admonitions. (Deut 11:18-19)
- We pray, by thanking and praising God for his grace and requesting healing for our bodies, minds, and souls. (Jer 10:25, Ps 128:3)
- We memorize scripture so that we might hide God's Word deep within our hearts. (Ps 119:11, Duet 6:6)
- We sing, by making a joyful noise, as a way to express our beliefs about God back to Him. (Ps 66:1-2, Col 3:16)
- We confess creeds and catechisms so we might organize our thoughts around what and why we believe.
- We teach to witness to our family so we can pass on the Goodness and Truth of the Bible (Ps 78:1-8, Eph 6:4)

It is that simple. There are no special keys to the definition of family worship. Family worship ought to be simple, thoughtful, and habitual.

Why do family worship?

Three reasons
1. Worship aligns our minds to the Gospel.
2. Prepares us for Sunday worship.
3. Excellent place to train our family in the Bible.

Daily worship aligns our priorities and minds toward the Gospel. By praying, singing, and reading with a joyful heart, we invite the Holy Spirit into our lives with great zeal.

Family worship mirrors our worship at church. That is,

- we confess what we believe back to God,
- we teach our family the truths of the Bible,
- we sing to remind our hearts of God's grace,
- we pray exultations and supplications to the Lord,
- and have a regular intake of the Bible.

Doing this daily contextualizes our minds into a mental space where we are constantly remembering the importance of God's grace, Jesus dying for our sins, and our part to play in this story.

If we want to live a Christlike life, seek to worship well on Sunday, and receive God's blessings, family worship is the life-giving breath to strengthen our souls.

A daily admonition from the Bible prepares our hearts for worship leading up to Sunday. This alone gives good reason to do family worship.

Finally, family worship is a natural and excellent way to train our family in the Bible. It solidifies how we worship on Sunday, enforces our Biblical understanding, and requires our time and attention. Thus, it's a natural training ground for getting better at reading, singing, praying, and discussing Gospel truths.

When and Where?

When and where each family chooses to do family worship will depend on each family's needs. Our family does it after dinner in the living room. Many families do it right at the dinner table.

The most important considerations for timing and location are consistency and practicality. You want your spouse, children, parents, and extended family members to remind each other of the chosen time and location for family worship.

Family worship does not have to be daily, but that should be the goal. The best habits are daily. Some families do it twice a day, once in the morning, once in the evening. Our family does it once in the evening.

Regardless of when and where you choose, it should be consistent and practical to strengthen the habit of doing.

The location should remind the family that one of the activities in that room is family worship. There may be chairs or spots on the floor that become natural locations to sit and participate.

The time should be preceded by something that brings the family together to ensure participation. The activities after should not be touched until the family has completed worship.

If you can stick to some simple rules, then this will become a natural, organic, and regular part of your family's day.

How to do family worship?

Daily family worship should be short, sweet, and purposeful according to the overall maturity of your family. If you have little kids, then short and small increments will be important. If you have older kids, then there should be room for lengthier discussions and longer singing.

It can take 5-30 minutes depending on what you want to incorporate. 10-15 minutes is usually a great balance. If it goes longer due to discussion or extra singing, that's ok. If it goes shorter because the reading is short and everyone needs to go to bed, that's ok.

Simple, steady, and consistent are how you lead your family in worship.

Mechanics of family worship

*Opening prayer*
Open worship with a prayer to center our hearts on eternal things. Ask that everyone would focus on worship, blocking out distractions, and turning our attention to God.
*Bible intake*
Reading the scripture is the first item. I would recommend reading through whole books and stories in the Bible. You can of course read sections and partial books if you prefer.

However, when doing Bible intake, it is helpful to ingest as large chunks as possible to help with context and fluidity.

If your children are small, it might behoove you to use a picture Bible in addition to the standard scripture reading. Children are apt to learn stories and lessons through listening. The more engaging the reading, the more they will actively listen.

*Discussion*
After reading, you may engage in a short discussion. Depending on the depth and breadth of the passage the discussion could be a summary of what was just read or a comment on how the passage applies to us.

It's helpful to point out one or two significant items from the passage for the family to dwell on. If you can engage in discussion, everyone will tend to absorb the message better.

*Memory / Training*
After Bible reading, you can engage in the work of memorizing scripture verses, creeds, or catechisms. This may not be of interest to everyone. But there is something powerful about having the ability to recall scripture and doctrinal truths whenever the heart leads us.

Memorizing provides a way to recall the Bible in times of need and joy. Training, practicing, and repeating creeds, catechisms, and scripture allow us to imbue our soul with life-giving water from God.

*Singing*
After training and memorization, we sing a hymn or worship song together. When learning a new song (particularly since our kids cannot read yet) we start with one verse and sign it twice through.

After a few days, add a second verse. Over time we all learn the lyrics and tunes.

As the family matures, adding live instruments to accompany the acapella singing would be an awesome expression of joy. Extending worship with multiple songs, according to your family's strengths, can be grown over time.

*Prayer*
Finally, we pray together to draw family worship to an end.

Prayers may consist of:
- Saying the Lord's Prayer collectively.
- One person following the ACTS model for the group.
- Each person taking a brief turn for supplications.
- Reading a Psalm and saying a prayer of reflection.
- Praying for illumination and consideration of our scripture reading.

Family Worship Example Routine

|  | Week 1 | | |
|---|---|---|---|
|  | Day 1 | Day 2 | Day 3 |
| Opening Prayer | Child leads. | Mom Leads. | Child Leads. |
| Bible | Read Scripture from the sermon. | Read Chapter 1 of Jonah. | Read Chapter 2 of Jonah. |
| Discuss | Discuss main sermon points. | Discuss Jonah's attitude toward God. | Discuss Jonah's response to his punishment. |
| Training | Recite the Apostles Creed as a family. | Catechism #4 | Catechism #4 |
| Sing | 1st verse of the hymn "For the Saints." | 1st verse of the hymn "For the Saints." | 1st verse of the hymn "For the Saints." |
| Prayer | Dad Leads in Supplication, takes request. | Dad Leads in ACTS prayer. | Mom leads in supplication takes requests. |

| | Week 1 | | | |
|---|---|---|---|---|
| | Day 4 | Day 5 | Day 6 | Day 7 |
| Opening Prayer | Dad leads. | Child Leads. | Child Leads. | Dad Leads. |
| Bible | Read Chapter 3 of Jonah. | Read Chapter 4 of Jonah. | Read Chapter 1 of Micah. | Read the passage from the last sermon. |
| Discuss | What it means to repent. | Discuss Jonah's attitude toward God. | Discuss the transgressions of a nation. | Discuss the main sermon points. |
| Training | Catechism #5. | Catechism #5. | Catechism #6. | Review Catechism #4, #5, and #6. |
| Sing | 1st and 2nd verses of "For the Saints." | 1st and 2nd verses of "For the Saints." | 1st and 2nd verses of "For the Saints." | 1st and 2nd verses of "For the Saints." |
| Prayer | Child leads in supplication, take requests. | Dad Leads in ACTS prayer. | Mom leads in ACTS prayer. | Child leads in the Lord's Prayer. |

Bible Reading

Reading Options

What's important about reading the Bible is taking in the Words of God and discussing this with our family.  Our family will pick up on nuances, concerns, and questions over time.

The goal is to grow the discussion over time.  Here are a few reading options.

1. If your children are young, there are a few Bible books with pictures that tell the stories of the Bible in simple ways.
2. Read the scripture passage from the previous Sermon at church or the next sermon at church.
3. Read through a book of the Bible section by section or chapter by chapter.
4. Read a section of scripture from this book.

Questions for discussion

Use these questions as a springboard for discussion, modify, add, and expound as your family needs.
- What does this passage remind us of?
- What can this passage tell us about the person of Christ?
- How does God illuminate the Gospel here?
- How do these characters of the Bible follow or reject God?
- How does this passage speak to our sin and need for a savior?
- Why do you think the author is saying these things?

Prayer

Opening Prayers

Below are some prayers to order your worship, please use and modify for your family.

*Lord, please order our family worship today, let us see and hear the Word of God.  Amen.*

*Dear Heavenly Father, speak to us your truths, let us honor you with our praise.  Amen.*

*God Almighty, we come to you with humble hearts, hear our praises.  Amen.*

*Lord of hosts, thank you for allowing us to worship and pray to you, bless our worship.  Amen.*

*Jesus, we thank you for your grace, make the words of our mouth honoring you.  Amen.*

*Our Lord and Savior, please guide our worship, use it to refine our hearts.  Amen.*

*Father in heaven, we ask that you would protect our hearts and minds as we set aside this time to worship you.  Amen*

*Lord of all, we give you our attention, please bless our words, songs, and prayers as we worship you.  Amen.*

The Lord's Prayer

Matthew 6: 9-13

9      Our Father in heaven,
hallowed be your name.

10     Your kingdom come,
your will be done,
on earth as it is in heaven.

11     Give us this day our daily bread,

12     and forgive us our debts,
as we also have forgiven our debtors.

13     And lead us not into temptation,
but deliver us from evil.

## ACTS - Prayer Model[1]

Simply follow this acronym when you pray. The sequencing of the prayer follows a natural path of humbling ourselves before God.

Adoration - Speak praises honoring our Lord God and Father.
- Great God and father, we worship and adore you, your grace abounds all around us. Your mercy is renewed every morning.
- Dear Heavenly Father, your creation calls out to you, through the winds on the seas, in storms and high mountains; your creation shows your awesome might.

Confession - Repent of your sins, calling out the need for Grace.
- We are humbled by your mercy. We are undeserving of your grace. We know we deserve hell. Forgive us of our sins, our sins of commission and omission. Forgive us for turning our back on you.
- Father, because we failed you, your Son, the Christ, died for our sins that we might be saved. We repent of our sins, we repent for putting idols before you Lord.

---

[1] The ACTS model of prayer has been around a long time and I have no idea who deserves attribution. I learned it by reading John Piper.

Thanksgiving - Thank God for Grace and Mercies; large and small.
- Oh Father in heaven, we thank you for our blessings, mercies, forgiveness, and grace.
- God, we are eternally grateful for your Son's death and resurrection, thank you for making us whole with you.

Supplication - Petitions and requests from our Father in Heaven.
- Lord, we ask that you would remind us of your grace that we might treat each other with kindness and thoughtfulness.
- Father, you tell us you are the Great Physician, we ask for healing of those who are unwell. Please stretch out your hand to health those whose souls are seeking your comfort.

Praying the Psalms

Option One.
- Select the Psalm (some people pray through them systematically).
- Read the Psalm in its entirety.
- Let your prayer reflect on the words of the Psalm by focusing on how they impact our hearts, actions, and thoughts.

Option Two
- Read the Psalm verse by verse.
- At the end of each verse, reflect with words out loud how you ought to interact, mirror, learn or apply the verse.
- When your reflection of that verse is completed, move onto the next verse, read and reflect.

Example.  Psalm in Bold, reflective words in *italics*.

Psalm 1
1 Blessed is the man who walks not in the counsel of the wicked, nor stands in the way of sinners, nor sits in the seat of scoffers;

*Lord, you tell us to follow Your words, not the words of others. Help us to listen and learn from your counsel only.*

2 but his delight is in the law of the Lord,
and on his law he meditates day and night.

*Our blessings abound when we seek Your will, we hope to have continuous joy in your Love.  Remind us to meditate on the Bible.*

Creeds

Introduction to Creeds

Creeds are a time-honored tradition of summarizing scriptural truths; also known as doctrine.  Creeds are brilliant tools for Christians to recall, understand, and memorize essential parts of the Christan faith.  These creeds have deep scriptural proof-texts and rich historical context.

The following creeds are still used today in various churches and traditions.  Except for the Nicene and Apostles creed, the remaining creeds are only represented partially.

Enjoy the abundance of these old words and the deeply thoughtful confessions of faith.

Learning a creed is taken in small pieces.  Start with one line.  Memorize it as a family.  Then add the second line.

Once you have the entire creed down, work the entire creed into a regular review.

Apostle's Creed

I believe in God, the Father Almighty,
the Maker of heaven and earth,
and in Jesus Christ, His only Son, our Lord:

Who was conceived by the Holy Ghost,
born of the virgin Mary, suffered under Pontius Pilate,
was crucified, dead, and buried;

He descended into hell.
The third day He arose again from the dead;

He ascended into heaven,
and sitteth on the right hand of God the Father Almighty;
from there he will come to judge the quick and the dead.

I believe in
the Holy Ghost;
the holy catholic church;
the communion of saints;
the forgiveness of sins;
the resurrection of the body;
and the life everlasting.

Amen.

The Nicene Creed

I believe in one God, the Father Almighty, Maker of heaven and earth, and of all things visible and invisible.

And in one Lord Jesus Christ, the only-begotten Son of God, begotten of the Father before all worlds; God of God, Light of Light, very God of very God; begotten, not made, being of one substance with the Father, by whom all things were made.

Who, for us men and for our salvation, came down from heaven, and was incarnate by the Holy Spirit of the virgin Mary, and was made man; and was crucified also for us under Pontius Pilate; He suffered and was buried; and the third day He rose again, according to the Scriptures; and ascended into heaven, and sits on the right hand of the Father; and He shall come again, with glory, to judge the quick and the dead; whose kingdom shall have no end.

And I believe in the Holy Ghost, the Lord and Giver of Life; who proceeds from the Father and the Son; who with the Father and the Son together is worshipped and glorified; who spoke by the prophets.

And I believe in one holy catholic and apostolic Church. I acknowledge one baptism for the remission of sins; and I look for the resurrection of the dead, and the life of the world to come.
Amen.

# The Scotts Confession

## Of God - Section 1

We confess and acknowledge one only God, to whom only we must cleave, whom only we must serve, whom only we must worship, and in whom only we must put our trust:

who is eternal, infinite, immeasurable, incomprehensible, omnipotent, invisible;

one in substance, and yet distinct in three persons: the Father, the Son, and the Holy Ghost;

by whom we confess and believe all things in heaven and in earth, as well visible as invisible, to have been created, to be retained in their being, and to be ruled and guided by his inscrutable Providence,

to such end as his eternal wisdom, goodness, and justice has appointed them, to the manifestation of his own glory.

The Belgic Confession

Of the Written Word of God - Section 7

We confess that this Word of God was not sent, nor delivered by the will of man, but that holy men of God spoke as they were moved by the Holy Ghost, as the apostle Peter says.

And that afterwards God, from a special care, which he has for us and our salvation, commanded his servants, the prophets and apostles, to commit his revealed word to writing; and he himself wrote with his own finger, the two tables of the law.

Therefore we call such writings holy and divine Scriptures.

The Heidelberg Catechism

First two questions.

Q. What is your only comfort in life and in death?

A. That I am not my own but belong— body and soul, in life and in death, to my faithful Savior, Jesus Christ.

He has fully paid for all my sins with his precious blood, and has set me free from the tyranny of the devil.

He also watches over me in such a way that not a hair can fall from my head without the will of my Father in heaven; in fact, all things must work together for my salvation.

Because I belong to him, Christ, by his Holy Spirit, assures me of eternal life and makes me wholeheartedly willing and ready from now on to live for him.

Q. What must you know to live and die in the joy of this comfort?

A. Three things:

First, how great my sin and misery are;
Second, how I am set free from all my sins and misery;
Third, how I am to thank God for such deliverance.

## Athanasian Creed

### Trinity: Sections 1-6

Whosoever will be saved, before all things it is necessary that he hold the catholic faith;

Which faith unless everyone does keep whole and undefiled, without doubt he shall perish everlastingly.

And the catholic faith is this: that we worship one God in Trinity, and Trinity in Unity;

Neither confounding the Persons, nor dividing the Essence.

For there is one Person of the Father; another of the Son; and another of the Holy Ghost.

But the Godhead of the Father, of the Son, and of the Holy Ghost, is all one; the Glory equal, the Majesty coeternal. Such as the Father is; such is the Son; and such is the Holy Ghost.

The Children's Catechism

## Introduction to Catechisms

Catechisms are time-tested, learning mechanisms for training adults and children on scriptural truths.  Catechisms are simply specific questions and answers designed to train people in the Bible as well as serving a summary of Biblical key truths and concepts.

All catechisms, like creeds, are backed with scriptural proof texts.

The Children's Catechisms are designed for, you guessed it, children although one could argue most adults could use the lessons from this particular set of questions.

These are most easily taught one at a time.  The entire family can and should learn them together.  It's helpful for everyone to have both the answer and question memorized.

Once you have a few down, once or twice a month, have a review as a refresher.

Q. 1. Who made you?
A. God.

Q. 2. What else did God make?
A. God made all things.

Q. 3. Why did God make you and all things?
A. For his own glory.

Q. 4. How can you glorify God?
A. By loving him and doing what he commands.

Q. 5. Why ought you to glorify God?
A. Because he made me and takes care of me.

Q. 6. Are there more gods than one?
A. There is only one God.

Q. 7. In how many persons does this one God exist?
A. In three persons.

Q. 8. What are they?
A. The Father, the Son, and the Holy Spirit.

Q. 9. What is God?
A. God is a Spirit, and does not have a body like men.

Q. 10. Where is God?
A. God is everywhere.

Q. 11. Can you see God?
A. No; I cannot see God, but he always sees me.

Q. 12. Does God know all things?
A. Yes; nothing can be hidden from God.

Q. 13. Can God do all things?
A. Yes; God can do all his holy will.

Q. 14. Where do you learn how to love and obey God?
A. In the Bible alone.

Q. 15. Who wrote the Bible?
A. Holy men who were taught by the Holy Spirit.

Q. 16. Who were our first parents?
A. Adam and Eve.

Q. 17. Of what were our first parents made?
A. God made the body of Adam out of the ground, and formed Eve from the body of Adam.

Q. 18. What did God give Adam and Eve besides bodies?
A. He gave them souls that could never die.

Q. 19. Do you have a soul as well as a body?
A. Yes; I have a soul that will never die.

Q. 20. How do you know that you have a soul?
A. Because the Bible tells me so.

Q. 21. In what condition did God make Adam and Eve?
A. He made them holy and happy.

Q. 22. What is a covenant?
A. An agreement between two or more persons.

Q. 23. What covenant did God make with Adam?
A. The covenant of works.

Q. 24. What was Adam bound to do by the covenant of works?
A. To obey God perfectly.

Q. 25. What did God promise in the covenant of works?
A. To reward Adam with life if he obeyed him.

Q. 26. What did God threaten in the covenant of works?
A. To punish Adam in eternity if he disobeyed.

Q. 27. Did Adam keep the covenant of works?
A. No; he sinned against God.

Q. 28. What is Sin?
A. Transgression of God's law.

Q. 29. What is a sin of omission?
A. Not being or doing what God requires.

Q. 30. What is a sin of commission?
A. Doing what God forbids.

Q. 31. What was the sin of our first parents?
A. Eating the forbidden fruit.

Q. 32. Who tempted them to this sin?
A. The devil tempted Eve, and she gave the fruit to Adam.

Q. 33. What befell our first parents when they had sinned?
A. Instead of being holy and happy, they became sinful and miserable.

Q. 34. Did Adam act for himself alone in the covenant of works?
A. No; he represented all his posterity.

Q. 35. What effect did the sin of Adam have on all mankind?
A. All mankind are born in a state of sin and misery.

Q. 36. What is the sinful nature which we inherit from Adam called?
A. Original sin.

Q. 37. What does every sin deserve?
A. The wrath and curse of God.

Q. 38. Can anyone go to heaven with this sinful nature?
A. No; our hearts must be changed before we can be fit for heaven.

Q. 39. What is a change of heart called?
A. Regeneration.

Q. 40. Who can change a sinner's heart?
A. The Holy Spirit alone.

Q. 41. Can anyone be saved through the covenant of works?
A. None can be saved through the covenant of works.

Q. 42. Why can none be saved through the covenant of works?
A. Because all have broken it, and are condemned by it

Q. 43. With whom did God the Father make the covenant of grace?
A. With Christ, his eternal Son.

Q. 44. Whom did Christ represent in the covenant of grace?
A. His elect people.

Q. 45. What did Christ undertake in the covenant of grace?
A. To keep the whole law for his people, and to suffer the punishment due to their sins.

Q. 46. Did our Lord Jesus Christ ever commit the least sin?
A. No; he was holy, harmless, and undefiled.

Q. 47. How could the Son of God suffer?
A. Christ, the Son of God, became man that he might obey and suffer in our nature.

Q. 48. What is meant by the Atonement?
A. Christ's satisfying divine justice, by his sufferings and death, in the place of sinners.

Q. 49. What did God the Father undertake in the covenant of grace?
A. To justify and sanctify those for whom Christ should die.

Q. 50. What is justification?
A. *It is God's forgiving sinners, and treating them as if they had never sinned.*

Q. 51. What is sanctification?
A. *It is God's making sinners holy in heart and conduct.*

Q. 52. For whom did Christ obey and suffer?
A. *For those whom the Father had given him.*

Q. 53. What kind of life did Christ live on earth?
A. *A life of poverty and suffering.*

Q. 54. What kind of death did Christ die?
A. *The painful and shameful death of the cross.*

Q. 55. Who will be saved?
A. *Only those who repent of sin, believe in Christ, and lead holy lives.*

Q. 56. What is it to repent?
A. *To be sorry for sin, and to hate and forsake it because it is displeasing to God.*

Q. 57. What is it to believe or have faith in Christ?
A. *To trust in Christ alone for salvation.*

Q. 58. Can you repent and believe in Christ by your own power?
A. *No; I can do nothing good without the help of God's Holy Spirit.*

Q. 59. How can you get the help of the Holy Spirit?
A. God has told us that we must pray to him for the Holy Spirit.

Q. 60. How long ago is it since Christ died?
A. More than nineteen hundred years.

Q. 61. How were pious persons saved before the coming of Christ?
A. By believing in a Savior to come.

Q. 62. How did they show their faith?
A. By offering sacrifices on God's altar.

Q. 63. What did these sacrifices represent?
A. Christ, the Lamb of God, who was to die for sinners.

Q. 64. What offices has Christ?
A. Christ has three offices.

Q. 65. What are they?
A. The offices of a prophet, of a priest, and of a king.

Q. 66. How is Christ a prophet?
A. Because he teaches us the will of God.

Q. 67. How is Christ a priest?
A. Because he died for our sins and pleads with God for us.

Q. 68. How is Christ a king?
A. Because he rules over us and defends us.

Q. 69. Why do you need Christ as a prophet?
A. *Because I am ignorant.*

Q. 70. Why do you need Christ as a priest?
A. *Because I am guilty.*

Q. 71. Why do you need Christ as a king?
A. *Because I am weak and helpless.*

Q. 72. How many commandments did God give on Mount Sinai?
A. *Ten commandments.*

Q. 73. What are the ten commandments sometimes called?
A. *The Decalogue.*

Q. 74. What do the first four commandments teach?
A. *Our duty to God.*

Q. 75. What do the last six commandments teach?
A. *Our duty to our fellow men.*

Q. 76. What is the sum of the ten commandments?
A. *To love God with all my heart, and my neighbor as myself.*

Q. 77. Who is your neighbor?
A. *All my fellow men are my neighbors.*

Q. 78. Is God pleased with those who love and obey him?
A. *Yes; he says, "I love them that love me."*

Q. 79. Is God displeased with those who do not love and obey him?
A. *Yes; "God is angry with the wicked every day."*

Q. 80. What is the first commandment?
A. The first commandment is, Thou shalt have no other gods before me.

Q. 81. What does the first commandment teach us?
A. To worship God alone.

Q. 82. What is the second commandment?
A. The second commandment is, Thou shalt not make unto thee any graven image, or any likeness of any things that is in heaven above, or that is in the earth beneath, or that is in the water under the earth; thou shalt not bow down thyself to them, nor serve them: for I, the Lord thy God, am a jealous God, visiting the iniquity of the fathers upon the children unto the third and fourth generation of them that hate me; and showing mercy unto thousands of them that love me, and keep my commandments.

Q. 83. What does the second commandment teach us?
A. To worship God in a proper manner, and to avoid idolatry.

Q. 84. What is the third commandment?
A. The third commandment is, Thou shalt not take the name of the Lord thy God in vain: for the Lord will not hold him guiltless that taketh his name in vain.

Q. 85. What does the third commandment teach me?
A. To reverence God's name, word, and works.

Q. 86. What is the fourth commandment?
A. The fourth commandment is, Remember the Sabbath day to keep it holy. Six days shalt thou labor, and do all thy work, but the seventh day is the Sabbath of the Lord thy God; in it thou shalt not do any work, thou, nor thy son, nor thy daughter, nor thy manservant, nor thy maidservant, nor thy cattle, nor thy stranger that is within thy gates: for in six days the Lord made heaven and earth, the sea, and all that in them is, and rested the seventh day; wherefore the Lord blessed the Sabbath Day, and hallowed it.

Q. 87. What does the fourth commandment teach us?
A. To keep the Sabbath holy.

Q. 88. What day of the week is the Christian Sabbath?
A. The first day of the week, called the Lord's day.

Q. 89. Why is it called the Lord's day?
A. Because on that day Christ rose from the dead.

Q. 90. How should the Sabbath be spent?
A. In prayer and praise, in hearing and reading God's Word, and in doing good to our fellow men.

Q. 91. What is the fifth commandment?
A. The fifth commandment is, Honor thy father and thy mother, that thy days may be long upon the land which the Lord thy God giveth thee.

Q. 92. What does the fifth commandment teach me?
A. To love and obey our parents and teachers.

Q. 93. What is the sixth commandment?
A. The sixth commandment is, Thou shalt not kill.

Q. 94. What does the sixth commandment teach us?
A. To avoid angry passions.

Q. 95. What is the seventh commandment?
A. The seventh commandment is, Thou shalt not commit adultery.

Q. 96. What does the seventh commandment teach us?
A. To be pure in heart, language, and conduct.

Q. 97. What is the eighth commandment?
A. The eighth commandment is, Thou shalt not steal.

Q. 98. What does the eighth commandment teach us?
A. To be honest and industrious.

Q. 99. What is the ninth commandment?
A. The ninth commandment is, Thou shalt not bear false witness against thy neighbor.

Q. 100. What does the ninth commandment teach us?
A. To tell the truth.

Q. 101. What is the tenth commandment?
A. The tenth commandment is, Thou shalt not covet thy neighbor's house, thou shalt not covet thy neighbor's wife, nor his manservant, nor his maidservant, nor his ox, nor his ass, nor anything that is thy neighbor's.

Q. 102. What does the tenth commandment teach us?
A. *To be content with our lot.*

Q. 103. Can any man keep these ten commandments perfectly?
A. *No mere man, since the fall of Adam, ever did or can keep the ten commandments perfectly.*

Q. 104. Of what use are the ten commandments to us?
A. *They teach us our duty, and show our need of a Savior.*

Q. 105. What is prayer?
A. *Prayer is asking God for things which he has promised to give.*

Q. 106. In whose name should we pray?
A. *Only in the name of Christ.*

Q. 107. What has Christ given us to teach us how to pray?
A. *The Lord's Prayer.*

Q. 108. Repeat the Lord's Prayer.
A. *Our Father in heaven, hallowed be your name. Your kingdom come, your will be done, on earth as it is in heaven. Give us this day our daily bread, and forgive us our debts, as we also have forgiven our debtors. And lead us not into temptation, but deliver us from evil.*

Q. 109. How many petitions are there in The Lord's Prayer?
A. *Six.*

Q. 110. What is the first petition?
A. *"Hallowed be thy name."*

Q. 111. What do we pray for in the first petition?
A. That God's name may be honored by us and all men.

Q. 112. What is the second petition?
A. "Thy kingdom come."

Q. 113. What do we pray for in the second petition?
A. That the gospel may be preached in all the world, and believed and obeyed by us and all men.

Q. 114. What is the third petition?
A. "Thy will be done in earth, as it is in heaven."

Q. 115. What do we pray for in the third petition?
A. That men on earth may serve God as the angels do in heaven.

Q. 116. What is the fourth petition?
A. "Give us this day our daily bread."

Q. 117. What do we pray for in the fourth petition?
A. That God would give us all things needful for our bodies and souls.

Q. 118. What is the fifth petition?
A. "And forgive us our debts, as we forgive our debtors."

Q. 119. What do we pray for in the fifth petition?
A. That God would pardon our sins for Christ's sake, and enable us to forgive those who have injured us.

Q. 120. What is the sixth petition?
A. "And lead us not into temptation, but deliver us from evil."

Q. 121. What do we pray for in the sixth petition?
A. That God would keep us from sin.

Q. 122. How many sacraments are there?
A. Two.

Q. 123. What are they?
A. Baptism and the Lord's Supper.

Q. 124. Who appointed these sacraments?
A. The Lord Jesus Christ.

Q. 125. Why did Christ appoint these sacraments?
A. To distinguish his disciples from the world, and to comfort and strengthen them.

Q. 126. What sign is used in baptism?
A. The washing with water.

Q. 127. What does this signify?
A. That we are cleansed from sin by the blood of Christ.

Q. 128. In whose name are we baptized?
A. In the name of the Father, and of the Son, and of the Holy Ghost.

Q. 129. Who are to be baptized?
A. Believers and their children.

Q. 130. Why should infants be baptized?
A. *Because they have a sinful nature and need a Savior.*

Q. 131. Does Christ care for little children?
A. *Yes; for he says, "Suffer the little children to come unto me, and forbid them not: for of such is the kingdom of God."*

Q. 132. To what does your baptism bind you?
A. *To be a true follower of Christ.*

Q. 133. What is the Lord's Supper?
A. *The eating of bread and drinking of wine in remembrance of the sufferings and death of Christ.*

Q. 134. What does the bread represent?
A. *The body of Christ, broken for our sins.*

Q. 135. What does the wine represent?
A. *The blood of Christ, shed for our salvation.*

Q. 136. Who should partake of the Lord's Supper?
A. *Only those who repent of their sins, believe in Christ for salvation, and love their fellow men.*

Q. 137. Did Christ remain in the tomb after his crucifixion?
A. *No; he rose from the tomb on the third day after his death.*

Q. 138. Where is Christ now?
A. *In heaven, interceding for sinners.*

Q. 139. Will he come again?
A. *Yes; at the last day Christ will come to judge the world.*

Q. 140. What becomes of men at death?
A. *The body returns to dust, and the soul goes into the world of spirits.*

Q. 141. Will the bodies of the dead be raised to life again?
A. *Yes; "The trumpet shall sound, and the dead shall be raised."*

Q. 142. What will become of the wicked in the day of judgment?
A. *They shall be cast into hell.*

Q. 143. What is hell?
A. *A place of dreadful and endless torment.*

Q. 144. What will become of the righteous?
A. *They shall be taken to heaven.*

Q. 145. What is heaven?
A. *A glorious and happy place, where the righteous shall be forever with the Lord.*

Scripture[2]

---

[2] The scripture passages are bold to reflect an option to read the text responsively. Meaning, one person reads the bold, the remaining group reads the non-bold.

The Ten Commandments

Exodus 20:1-17

1       And God spoke all these words, saying,

2       **I am the Lord your God, who brought you out of the land of Egypt, out of the house of slavery.**

3       You shall have no other gods before me.

4       **You shall not make for yourself a carved image, or any likeness of anything that is in heaven above, or that is in the earth beneath, or that is in the water under the earth.**

5       You shall not bow down to them or serve them, for I the Lord your God am a jealous God, visiting the iniquity of the fathers on the children to the third and the fourth generation of those who hate me,

6       **but showing steadfast love to thousands of those who love me and keep my commandments.**

7       You shall not take the name of the Lord your God in vain, for the Lord will not hold him guiltless who takes his name in vain.

8       **Remember the Sabbath day, to keep it holy.**

9       Six days you shall labor, and do all your work,

10   but the seventh day is a Sabbath to the Lord your God. On it you shall not do any work, you, or your son, or Your daughter, your male servant, or your female servant, or your livestock, or the sojourner who is within your gates.

11   For in six days the Lord made heaven and earth, the sea, and all that is in them, and rested on the seventh day. Therefore the Lord blessed the Sabbath day and made it holy.

12   **Honor your father and your mother, that your days may be long in the land that the Lord your God is giving you.**

13   You shall not murder.

14   **You shall not commit adultery.**

15   You shall not steal.

16   **You shall not bear false witness against your neighbor.**

17   You shall not covet your neighbor's house; you shall not covet your neighbor's wife, or his male servant, or his female servant, or his ox, or his donkey, or anything that is your neighbor's.

## The Greatest Commandment

Matthew 22:36-40

36  "Teacher, which is the great commandment in the Law?"

37  **And he said to him, "You shall love the Lord your God with all your heart and with all your soul and with all your mind.**

38  This is the great and first commandment.

39  **And a second is like it: You shall love your neighbor as yourself.**

40  On these two commandments depend all the Law and The Prophets."

The Great Commission

Matthew 28:16-20

16   Now the eleven disciples went to Galilee, to the Mountain to which Jesus had directed them.

17   **And when they saw him they worshiped him, but some doubted.**

18   And Jesus came and said to them, "All authority in Heaven and on earth has been given to me.

19   **Go therefore and make disciples of all nations, baptizing them in the name of the Father and of the Son and of the Holy Spirit,**

20   teaching them to observe all that I have commanded You. And behold, I am with you always, to the end of the age."

**The Fruit of the Spirit**

Galatians 5:22-23

22 But the fruit of the Spirit is love, joy, peace, patience, kindness, goodness, faithfulness,

23 **gentleness, self-control; against such things there is no law.**

The Creation of the World

Genesis 1:1-5

1   In the beginning, God created the heavens and the earth.

2   **The earth was without form and void, and darkness was over the face of the deep. And the Spirit of God was hovering over the face of the waters.**

3   And God said, "Let there be light," and there was light.

4   **And God saw that the light was good. And God Separated the light from the darkness.**

5   God called the light Day, and the darkness he called Night. And there was evening and there was morning, the first day.

**Prophecy of Christ's Birth**

Isaiah 9:6-7

6   For to us a child is born,
    to us a son is given;
    and the government shall be upon his shoulder,
    and his name shall be called
    Wonderful Counselor, Mighty God,
    Everlasting Father, Prince of Peace.

7   **Of the increase of his government and of peace there will be no end,
    on the throne of David and over his kingdom,
    to establish it and to uphold it
    with justice and with righteousness
    from this time forth and forevermore.
    The zeal of the Lord of hosts will do this.**

## The Birth of Jesus Christ

Matthew 1:18-23

18  Now the birth of Jesus Christ took place in this way. When his mother Mary had been betrothed to Joseph, before they came together she was found to be with child from the Holy Spirit.

19  **And her husband Joseph, being a just man and unwilling to put her to shame, resolved to divorce her quietly.**

20  But as he considered these things, behold, an angel of The Lord appeared to him in a dream, saying, "Joseph, son of David, do not fear to take Mary as your wife, for that which is conceived in her is from the Holy Spirit.

21  **She will bear a son, and you shall call his name Jesus, for he will save his people from their sins."**

22  All this took place to fulfill what the Lord had spoken by The prophet:

23  **"Behold, the virgin shall conceive and bear a son, and They shall call his name Immanuel" (which means, God with us).**

24  When Joseph woke from sleep, he did as the angel of The Lord commanded him: he took his wife,

25  **but knew her not until she had given birth to a son. And he called his name Jesus.**

## Testing of Your Faith

James 1:2-6

2   Count it all joy, my brothers, when you meet trials of various kinds,

3   **for you know that the testing of your faith produces steadfastness.**

4   And let steadfastness have its full effect, that you may be perfect and complete, lacking in nothing.

5   **If any of you lacks wisdom, let him ask God, who gives generously to all without reproach, and it will be given him.**

6   But let him ask in faith, with no doubting, for the one who doubts is like a wave of the sea that is driven and tossed by the wind.

**John's Prophecy of Christ**

John 1:1-9

1 In the beginning was the Word, and the Word was with God, and the Word was God.

2 **He was in the beginning with God.**

3 All things were made through him, and without him was not anything made that was made.

4 **In him was life and the life was the light of men.**

5 The light shines in the darkness, and the darkness has not overcome it.

6 **There was a man sent from God, whose name was John.**

7 He came as a witness, to bear witness about the light, that all might believe through him.

8 **He was not the light, but came to bear witness about the light.**

9 The true light, which gives light to everyone, was coming into the world.

The Whole Armor of God

Ephesians 6: 10-20

10   Finally, be strong in the Lord and in the strength of his might.

11   **Put on the whole armor of God, that you may be able to stand against the schemes of the devil.**

12   For we do not wrestle against flesh and blood, but Against the rulers, against the authorities, against the Cosmic powers over this present darkness, against the Spiritual forces of evil in the heavenly places.

13   **Therefore take up the whole armor of God, that you may be able to withstand in the evil day, and having done all, to stand firm.**

14   Stand therefore, having fastened on the belt of truth, and having put on the breastplate of righteousness,

15   **and, as shoes for your feet, having put on the Readiness given by the gospel of peace.**

16   In all circumstances take up the shield of faith, with which you can extinguish all the flaming darts of the evil one;

17   **and take the helmet of salvation, and the sword of the**

**Spirit, which is the word of God,**

18   praying at all times in the Spirit, with all prayer and supplication. To that end, keep alert with all perseverance, making supplication for all the saints,

19   **and also for me, that words may be given to me in Opening my mouth boldly to proclaim the mystery of the gospel,**

20   for which I am an ambassador in chains, that I ma Declare it boldly, as I ought to speak.

**Return to the Lord**

Joel 2:12-13

12   Even now, declares the LORD, "return to me with all your heart, with fasting and weeping and mourning."

13   **Rend your heart and not your garments. Return to the LORD your God, for he is gracious and compassionate, slow to anger and abounding in love, and he relents from sending calamity.**

Approved Worker

2nd Timothy 2:22-26

22    So flee youthful passions and pursue righteousness, Faith, love, and peace, along with those who call on the Lord From a pure heart.

23    **Have nothing to do with foolish, ignorant Controversies; you know that they breed quarrels.**

24    And the Lord's servant must not be quarrelsome but kind to everyone, able to teach, patiently enduring evil,

25    **correcting his opponents with gentleness. God may perhaps grant them repentance leading to a knowledge of the truth,**

26    and they may come to their senses and escape from the snare of the devil, after being captured by him to do his will.

## Psalm 1

1 Blessed is the man who walks not in the counsel of the wicked, nor stands in the way of sinners, nor sits in the seat of scoffers;

2 **but his delight is in the law of the Lord,
and on his law he meditates day and night.**

3 He is like a tree planted by streams of water that yields its fruit in its season, and its leaf does not wither. In all that he does, he prospers.

4 **The wicked are not so,
but are like chaff that the wind drives away.**

5 Therefore the wicked will not stand in the judgment, nor sinners in the congregation of the righteous;

6 **for the Lord knows the way of the righteous,
but the way of the wicked will perish.**

## Psalm 23

The Lord Is My Shepherd.  A Psalm of David.

1      The Lord is my shepherd; I shall not want.

2      **He makes me lie down in green pastures.**
        **He leads me beside still waters.**

3      He restores my soul.
        He leads me in paths of righteousness
        for his name's sake.

4      **Even though I walk through the valley of the shadow of death**
        **I will fear no evil, for you are with me;**
        **your rod and your staff, they comfort me.**

5      You prepare a table before me
        in the presence of my enemies;
        you anoint my head with oil;
        my cup overflows.

6      **Surely goodness and mercy shall follow my**
        **all the days of my life,**
        **and I shall dwell in the house of the Lord forever.**

Psalm 103:8-12

8   The Lord is merciful and gracious,
    slow to anger and abounding in steadfast love.

9   **He will not always chide,
    nor will he keep his anger forever.**

10  He does not deal with us according to our sins,
    nor repay us according to our iniquities.

11  **For as high as the heavens are above the earth,
    so great is his steadfast love toward those who fear him;**

12  as far as the east is from the west,
    so far does he remove our transgressions from us.

Psalm 117

1     **The Lord's Faithfulness Endures Forever**
Praise the Lord, all nations! Extol him, all peoples!

2     **For great is his steadfast love toward us,
and the faithfulness of the Lord endures forever.
Praise the Lord!**

## Psalm 121

My Help Comes from the Lord.  A Song of Ascents.

1    I lift up my eyes to the hills.
From where does my help come?

2    **My help comes from the Lord,**
**who made heaven and earth.**

3    He will not let your foot be moved;
he who keeps you will not slumber.

4    **Behold, he who keeps Israel**
**will neither slumber nor sleep.**

5    The Lord is your keeper;
the Lord is your shade on your right hand.

6    **The sun shall not strike you by day,**
**nor the moon by night.**

7    The Lord will keep you from all evil;
he will keep your life.

8    **The Lord will keep**
**your going out and your coming in**
**from this time forth and forevermore.**

Psalm 150

1	Let Everything Praise the Lord. Praise the Lord!
	Praise God in his sanctuary; praise him in his mighty heavens!

2	**Praise him for his mighty deeds;**
	**praise him according to his excellent greatness!**

3	Praise him with trumpet sound;
	praise him with lute and harp!

4	**Praise him with tambourine and dance;**
	**praise him with strings and pipe!**

5	Praise him with sounding cymbals;
	praise him with loud clashing cymbals!

6	**Let everything that has breath praise the Lord!**
	**Praise the Lord!**

Singing

Introduction to Singing

Not everyone is naturally good at singing.  It's a talent and skill.  If we regularly worship at church we can use our weekly practice on Sunday as a working model to mirror.  If your church sings hymns, then practice singing hymns at home.  If your church sings praise and worship songs, then start with some tunes you already know.

Singing acapella might be challenging, but it's not impossible.  If anyone in your family can play an instrument for accompaniment all the better.

There are many websites to help with tunes, sheet music, or ideas.

Keep it simple, start with singing one verse or one song a night.  Add and adjust over time.

There are two songs included, both are standards for closing worship services.

## Doxology

Praise God from whom all blessings flow
Praise him all creatures here below
Praise him above ye heavenly hosts
Praise father, son, and holy ghost


## Gloria Patri

Glory be to the Father,
and to the Son, and to the Holy Ghost;
as it was in the beginning,
is now, and ever shall be,
world without end. Amen, amen.

# Appendix

## I: How do I start?

Getting started is as easy as telling your family you want to try something new after dinner.

You tell everyone to sit down, explain to them this is an experiment until we figure out how to do it. Let them know the Holy Spirit has laid this on your heart and worshipping God daily seems like a wonderful way to celebrate His righteousness and admonish the family in God's Holiness.

You can then explain the parts of family worship. If you feel uncomfortable with something, just leave it out, and add it later.

Then you pray to open worship.

Then read a passage from scripture. Ask if anyone has any questions.

Pick a familiar song or hymn. Sing one verse.

Pray the Lord's prayer out loud.

Look around and thank everyone for participating. Let everyone know we'll do this again tomorrow and you might change or add things as the family becomes more practiced.

That's it. 5 mins to start. Build around that. Just do it tomorrow. And the following day and the next. Build the habit.

## II: Evolving Worship Over Time

*Phase I: Habit building*
To get your family started, it's about building a habit. Strengthening a muscle. Getting everyone to sit down and spend time before God. That's it.

*Phase II: Discussion, Catechizing, Memorization*
Once the habit is built, the goals should be about opening up opportunities to have discussions with the family. Reading deeply and asking questions to drive the conversation is not always natural, but it is necessary to grow our appreciation of the Gospel.

To deepen training, the family will also want to focus on the memorization of scripture, creeds, and catechisms.

*Phase III: Deep and Critical Discussions*
The goal is to explain, explore, and solidify core principles and application of the Gospel in all scenarios.

When we take time to probe, re-read, re-think, critically understand, and discuss with nuance, we get deeper into understanding and applying the Bible. It is during these times of spiritual fellowship, with our family, we strengthen life long bonds between each other and the Holy Spirit.

**Developing complexity over time.**

Consider the following graph.  This graph is anecdotal.

The goal is to start in the lower left quadrant and over time, move slowly, into the upper right quadrant.  There's no telling how long or how complex the worship, singing, prayer, study, and memorization, can get, but ideally, the family, as a whole, becomes more engaged and mature in how they present worship before God.

This is not a goal, rather, an illustration to show where to start and where you may end up.  Enjoy the process, embrace the Holy Spirit, and worship with diligence.

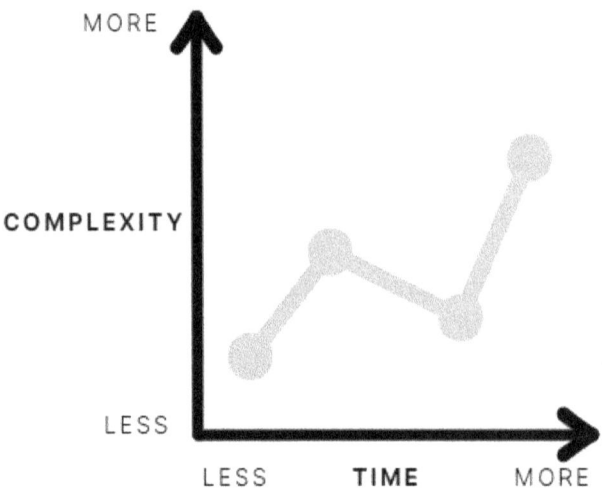

## III: Common Objections

**Our family does not have time.** That is fair, we live in a busy day and age. Family worship is just like anything else. We either choose to put other idols before God or we put God before the pleasures of this world. Carve out the time by prioritizing 15 minutes every day. Remember, it's a privilege, not a chore.

**Not everyone can get together at the same time.** This is tricky, various age ranges of kids, different work schedules, and complicated family scenarios abound. Unfortunately, the only practical advice here is to find the very limited time when the family is together and use that time. Again, it comes down to priority. Pray about this, ask God to find your family more time together.

**My kids are to spread apart in age.** This is a common issue. Most little kids can do what the older kids can do. The biggest issue is attention span. So, allow longer discussion for older kids and allow the younger kids to wiggle and move around. But keep everyone engaged as best possible. We are all in various seasons of life. We simply need to do our best to worship God habitually. It will never be perfect.

**I'm not spiritually mature enough.** Let me take a minute with this objection. No one really feels worthy to worship God. It's part of our fallen nature. It can be a temptation to use our lack of spiritual maturity. Or use our own poor devotional life, as a reason we cannot lead our family. But, as one of my favorite pastor's says, "that is a lie from the pit of Hell."

Reference Corithinians 10:13 "No temptation has overtaken you that is not common to man. God is faithful, and he will not let you be tempted beyond your ability, but with the temptation he will also provide the way of escape, that you may be able to endure it." God has given us tools to tackle this responsibility.

God has no expectations that we will do anything in this life perfectly. He's already handled that for us with the Atoning blood of Christ.

So, the best we can do……is…… the best we can do.

Trust God in the tools and faculties we are blessed with. Sing, Pray, Read, and memorize. You will be ok.

**A Final Note to the family worship leader.** This part is hard to write. I am exactly as broken as my sin has made me and I am exactly as saved by grace as God has willed. To lead in front, means to be in error publically in front of your family.

It means, when I lose my cool, or control of my tongue, I am now compelled to show my belief in God's grace in front of everyone. I need to apologize, ask for forgiveness, and be reconciled with God and my family. It can be hard, but it is a part of God's sanctifying plan for us.

So what I'm saying is, when we feel unable, unworthy, uncomfortable, or somehow hobbled, we should be humbled by our very real Grace from God and lead with confidence. This is your calling.

## IV: Bibliography

Whitney, D. S. (2015). Praying the Bible. Wheaton, IL: Crossway.

Whitney, D. S. (2016). Family worship. Wheaton, IL: Crossway.

Beeke, J. R. (2008). The family at church: Listening to sermons and attending prayer meetings. Grand Rapids, MI, MI: Reformation Heritage Books.

Beeke, J. R. (2009). Family worship. Grand Rapids, MI: Reformation Heritage Books.

Schaff, P., & Schaff, P. (1931). The Creeds of Christendom. New York: Harper.

Lloyd-Jones, S., & Jago. (2017). *The Jesus storybook Bible: Every story whispers his name.* Grand Rapids, MI: Zonderkidz.

Henley, K. (2005). *The beginner's bible: Timeless children's stories.* Grand Rapids, MI: Zondervan.

## V: Further Resources

For additional resources, head over to zackfink.com. There you will find other resources, books, links, and courses.

If this book was helpful but you would like more information, please check out my course with the same title, "Simple Family Worship," zackfink.com/simplefamilyworship.

I hope this book was helpful, please leave a review on Amazon if you found it relevant to you and your family's walk with God. Feedback is appreciated!

www.ingramcontent.com/pod-product-compliance
Lightning Source LLC
Chambersburg PA
CBHW032207040426
42449CB00005B/470